LAZY LAMA LOOKS AT

Buddhist
Meditation

RINGU TULKU RINPOCHE

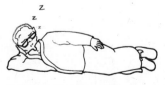

Number 1 in the Lazy Lama series

Bodhicharya
PUBLICATIONS
Awaken the heart by opening the mind

First Published in 1998 by
Bodhicharya Publications
24 Chester Street, Oxford, OX4 1SN, United Kingdom.
www.bodhicharya.org   email: publications@bodhicharya.org

ISBN 978-0-9576398-1-2

Second Edition. 2013.

First transcribed and edited by Cait Collins 1998.

Typesetting & Design by Paul O'Connor at Judo Design, Ireland.

Printed on recycled paper by Imprint Digital, Devon, UK.

Cover Image: © Dr Dirk de Klerk
Internal illustrations: Robin Bath
Lazy Lama logo: Dr Conrad Harvey & Rebecca O'Connor

Editor's Preface

This booklet on Buddhist Meditation is the first in the Lazy Lama series of short teachings by Ringu Tulku. It is the text of a talk given in Cambridge in the summer of 1997 at the request of students of Chime Rinpoche.

The biggest difficulty in editing transcripts of talks lies in trying to convey the flavour of the distinctive qualities of the live presentation, with all the tones and the expressions and gestures and the body language - the living presence of the person - on the printed page. Ringu Tulku brings his own very special warmth and kindness and humour to his teachings, and I hope these qualities come through in the following pages.

Cait Collins
1998

The basis for Buddhist practice

People sometimes think that meditation is all there is to Buddhism but I really don't agree with that: meditation is a very important part, but it is not everything.

I see Buddhist practice as being a way to work on yourself, to try to improve yourself. Somebody once asked me, 'What is the one thing you have to believe if you want to become a Buddhist, without which you could not become a Buddhist?'

It was an interesting question, and I thought a lot about how to answer it. First I thought maybe it was believing in the Buddha, Dharma, and Sangha; believing in taking refuge in these three. But I don't think that is the case: that comes later on. When somebody becomes a Buddhist they don't need to believe in the Buddha, Dharma and Sangha; they don't even know what they are. You need to traverse the entire path of Buddhism to know that - all of Buddhism is to try to understand that - so you can't make it a condition for becoming a Buddhist. Then what is it? I think it is to have the thought: I can change, I can improve; I can develop my positive qualities.' I think that's the basis. If you don't believe you can improve then I think there is no basis for becoming a Buddhist, or doing any Buddhist practice.

It is really all that's necessary, because taking refuge in Buddha, Dharma and Sangha is based on the understanding that I can improve, I can increase my wisdom, my compassion, my happiness, my joy; I can improve all these positive qualities - not just a little, but almost limitlessly. And from a Buddhist point of view that is enlightenment; that is buddhahood. A buddha is somebody who has improved his or her positive side, her own inherent good nature, to its ultimate level. That is a buddha. So a Buddhist is somebody who believes that he or she can improve, and improve really completely to become a buddha. Therefore that is the practice of Buddhism: to improve ourselves.

So, if I want to improve myself, meditation is a very important part of my practice, but there are also other aspects to it. Traditionally, Buddhist practice may be seen in terms of three aspects: view, meditation, and action.

The Buddhist way of understanding

The first one, view, is a way of understanding: we try to understand and perceive reality more clearly; we try to see what is wrong with our usual way of perceiving and reacting to the world. In Buddhism it is regarded as very important to gain insight, to see things clearly, and to work on our confusion.

It is even thought that the basis of all our problems is in fact a misunderstanding: the basis of all our sufferings, of all our negative emotions, all our conflicting and disturbing thoughts and feelings, is in fact a very powerful misunderstanding. Sometimes this misunderstanding is called ignorance: ignorance, because we don't see clearly for all the confusion.

It's the unclear view, being unable to see things as they really are. Because we can't see things as they really are we conceptualise and interpret; we identify and designate and thereby we separate; we impose our own concepts and imputations on things in such a way that we create our aversion and attachment. We make some things out to be very nice and others very bad, and then we try to go after those we have imputed to be nice and to avoid those we have imputed to be bad. And because it's always our own imputation we can't get out of it; we're entangled in it.

All these problems are due to our own mistaken way of perception, our own misunderstanding, which has been stabilised and confirmed and made strong and solid by our habitual tendencies for so long that we have become more and more entangled in it. It has become our established pattern of perception and reaction and we can't get out of it.

So, it's regarded as very important to try to understand this as being the basic problem. But even if we try to understand and analyse, and we try to see things more clearly, that by itself doesn't change our way of feeling. Although we might understand that it's not good to be angry, for instance, we still find ourselves getting angry. We're trying to achieve some understanding, but that's not enough; so what else can we do? This is where meditation comes in.

Taking understanding to a deeper level

Meditation is a way of trying to get deeper into ourselves; it allows us to reach a more subtle level of mind and is a way to familiarise

ourselves with our understanding. Usually
our understanding is at an intellectual level;
it's conceptual; so now we need to try to
get this understanding deep into our being,
to so familiarise ourselves with it that it
becomes a part of us, so we just become that
understanding. To do that we need meditation.

This kind of meditation is called
insight meditation; in Tibetan Ihak-tong
(lhag-mthong), or in Sanskrit vipashana

(vipasyana). We try to prepare to understand deeply, prepare to have this deep experience - not just the understanding in the head but the experiential understanding - which is called insight. Before we can do this we will need to practice another kind of meditation, the calming-down meditation or calm-abiding meditation; in Tibetan shi-nay (zhi-gnas), or in Sanskrit shamata (samatha). In this calm-abiding kind of meditation we are simply trying to learn how to be. I think the whole of meditation is actually learning how to be, but especially so in calm-abiding meditation. There are many different kinds of meditation in Buddhist practice, but all of them can be categorised into just these two: calm-abiding and insight meditation.

Calming the mind

The Tibetan word, shi-nay, which is translated into English as 'calm-abiding', has two parts:

shi, meaning calm, peace, or peaceful, and nay, which means resting or abiding. These two aspects of the meaning are reflected in how we go about practising this kind of meditation.

First we try to rest the mind, to create a state of relaxation, a state of freedom in the mind; to create a sense of being at ease in our mind. Until we can do that we don't have the environment or ground in which insight can arise because we are too tense and too busy; we are so restless that we have no space. So we are trying here to be a little bit restful, peaceful, at ease and relaxed.

This relaxation doesn't necessarily mean not doing anything, like sunbathing on the beach; in fact we could be sunbathing and still have tension and restlessness. Nor is it like yachting! I used to think that yachting must be the most restful thing, because I had seen pictures of yachts sailing along with the people on them sleeping, and with food and drink and everything you could want all around. But it's only like that in pictures! When I actually went sailing I discovered it wasn't restful at all; it was hard work all the time - there was no lying down, everybody was running around! I almost broke my head on the boom! I said, 'You call this leisure?!' And they said, 'Well sometimes if the wind is right and the weather is very good then you can just let it go; sometimes; once in a blue moon!' Meditation is not that kind of resting, but a real resting from within; a being at ease, so you don't need to feel tense all the time.

So one might say this calm-abiding meditation is the most important preparation: it's regarded not as an end but as a means, as a stepping stone leading to insight; it's not the final goal, but it's a very important step.

This meditation is traditionally done with time and with space. We try to make some time in our everyday life, either in the morning or evening or whenever we can, to create a peaceful state in which to train ourselves. It may be quite short: fifteen minutes, twenty minutes, half an hour; or one or two hours - whatever time we have, we try to create a space and a time where we can learn how to relax and how to be and how to allow ourselves to be calm and clear.

The more our mind is relaxed and at ease, the more peaceful it becomes; and the more peaceful it becomes the more clear it becomes. From a Buddhist point of view, when the mind becomes clear then the other good qualities of the mind can come through: if our mind becomes calm and thereby clear, then we can see more clearly; for example, we can see beyond the usual restrictions of time and space. We believe such qualities as telepathy, becoming sensitive to others' minds, and seeing events in far places emerge as a result of the mind's becoming clear. And not only these kinds of qualities of clarity but also all the positive qualities, such as wisdom and compassion, are naturally there. In fact that's the main Buddhist philosophy, especially of Vajrayana and Mahayana Buddhism, that the improvement we were talking about is not a result of our adding something to what we already have, but has always been there as part of our intrinsic nature, as its inseparable quality.

Buddha-nature

This is why Buddhists say that every sentient being has buddha-nature. What this means is that at the root of the being of each one of us, our mind - and here I don't mean only the thinking mind or consciousness but the totality of our experience - is basically not only pure, but also has all the positive qualities: the compassion and wisdom and joy, the clarity and ability to see things clearly - it's all there. It's just covered up: we can't see it at the moment because of its obscuration by our own misunderstanding and our habitual tendencies, but if we can relax in it and let it be unveiled then it just appears and all the good qualities emerge.

From a Buddhist point of view, if you can just be, really be, in your true natural state then all these good qualities are already there; so you don't need to try to do something to make yourself joyful, for example - if you can really be yourself the joyfulness manifests on its own. That's the Buddhist way of thinking, that basically you are all right, and everything which is not all right is a temporary accretion, something added which can be washed away.

Being natural

Just as the extra layers are mainly our own added-on concepts and assumptions, our theories and identifications and imputations, so meditation is basically learning a way to just be, to just be natural, without all these added conceptual extras. But this being natural doesn't mean just going along with our habitual tendencies.

There are two different ways of being natural. Being natural according to our habitual tendencies is the way we usually know how to be, more or less: we relax and we think, 'Oh, let's go for a drink,' or we relax and then we need to smoke a cigarette, because that is our habitual tendency. When we are talking about the basic nature from a Buddhist point of view, we're not talking about that kind of habitual basic nature, as in the sense that people are generally competitive, generally jealous, generally angry; that may be natural in the habitual tendency way, but it is not the deeper basic nature.

I remember seeing a film in which some children were stranded on an island, and the children, although they were very young, were shown as already having the traits of jealousy and competitiveness; they were fighting and so on. Of course they were: that is the habitual tendency kind of nature. Even the very moment we are born - and here this accords with the Buddhist belief in rebirth - we have habitual tendencies.

But that's not the basic nature we're talking about: there is a deeper way of being natural, beyond that. The deepest, completely basic true nature, according to Buddhism, is pure. So we try to go back to that state, to our very basic true nature. And how to do that, from a Buddhist point of view, is through learning how to be, just be; and that is the meditation.

Meditation posture

Meditation starts by learning step by step. First we try to relax our body, and for this a standard sitting position is sometimes explained.

The body is important. It's not the case that the body, mind and soul are three completely separate things. Sometimes when a strong emotion arises, people say, 'Oh it's really physical; it's not mental, it's physical.' Of course it's physical. When something happens in the mind, it is physical: when you are angry your face becomes red; when you are sad, tears come out; that's physical. And that's why when the body is affected the mind is also affected.

The connection between the mind and body is very strong; they are almost inseparable; therefore it is believed that establishing the right body posture helps the mind to settle down. So the meditation starts with taking up a certain body posture. Some people go to the extreme of saying that if you have the right body posture you don't have to do anything else, as the meditation will automatically follow, but I don't know whether this is really to be taken literally; sometimes this sort of thing may be said to emphasise the importance of a point.

However, we start with the body posture: sitting, and with a straight back; the straight back is said to be most important. Although traditionally we sit cross-legged, I don't think that can be so essential, because in all the drawings and images of the future Buddha, Buddha Maitreya, he is portrayed sitting on a chair! This hasn't just happened in the last few centuries but was done right from the time whenever the first image was made: the future Buddha is sitting on a chair. So maybe it's not too bad to sit on a chair! Maybe those of us who can't sit on a chair comfortably will not be born when the future Buddha comes! Once you get used to it, sitting cross-legged is very comfortable. Then you won't be able to sit on a chair; it will become very difficult! I've been sitting on chairs all my life, but still I'm not comfortable on a chair, and as soon as I get a chance I get down! But I think it is all right to sit on a chair. And then you sit with your back straight, and the body not leaning to either side or forwards or backwards; and your neck also not either side or forwards or backwards; and then the face also, a little bit softened, and not too much tension; and the teeth not grinding or clenched, and the lips relaxed.

Sitting properly is a way of releasing the tension. When we look at somebody meditating - or even not meditating also – we can see how the person is, can't we? We can see how their mind is, by looking at the face: he's tense, or she's not tense. They say the face is like the door of the mind. So relaxing the face is important. By relaxing the mind maybe your face relaxes, but relaxing the face also helps to relax the mind. And then the eyes are important: it's said that if you can relax your eyes then you can relax everything. So you need to be relaxed but straight - because if you are not straight then you will soon become unbalanced. A balanced and relaxed posture is the starting point.

Feeling at ease

Feeling at ease is the most important thing. Sometimes people even suggest you should try to almost artificially create a feeling of relaxation, of feeling good, feeling comfortable, to 'feel as if all the cells of your body are smiling.' How would you feel if all the cells of your body were smiling? It would feel very nice, wouldn't it?

That's the thing: feeling nice. Feeling nice is very important because, from a Buddhist point of view, the more you become habituated to feel a certain way, the more you become like that. That's the learning process. The more relaxed you feel, the more relaxed you become; the more natural you feel the more natural you become; the more joyful you feel the more joyful you become. And in the same way, the more angry you are the more angry you become, or the more miserable you are the more miserable you become. It's all habit. So here we're trying to relax; because once you feel nice - as if all the cells of your body are smiling - then there's no need to feel bad, no need to feel tense.

Thoughts and feelings

And now for the mind. Put the mind in the same way: just let the mind be relaxed. Of course, it won't stay that way. That's the problem! The mind will run; the mind will jump. According to modern science we've evolved from monkeys, so maybe that's why we have the habit of the monkey-mind, jumping about!

This is where we need some technique. What should we do? Should we say, 'Quiet! Quiet! Quiet!'? It won't be quiet. If you say, 'Not so much thinking; stop thinking,' it won't stop, will it? The more you try, the worse it becomes! That's why meditation becomes so difficult: because if you just try to stop your thoughts and stop your tension you

can't do it; the more you try, the more tense you become. But there must be a way to do it. And this is the important part, the main thing to learn: that you can't say 'Stop thinking,' and it will stop. You just have to let it be.

We can't shut off our mind. So when thoughts come and emotions come we have to learn a way to let things be; or to let things go, you can say. You can't do anything but let it come up, because it comes up; but then if you follow it you'll just go all over everywhere and there will be no meditation. So what can we do?

This is the key. When a thought comes up, we let it come up and then we let it go. How to do that? We just let it be. We do only one thing: we don't follow that thought.

The thought comes up, and we let it come up, but then we don't get entangled with it and run around after it. We don't say, 'This thought's no good; I shouldn't have this thought'; nor do we say, 'Oh that's a good thought; it's good to have that thought.' We just don't say anything.

It's as though somebody is entering an empty house: when somebody enters an empty house, there's nothing there to be taken away, nothing to be disturbed, so they just come in and go out; it doesn't matter. That's the way to react with the thoughts: just let them be. A thought comes in and goes out, and we say, 'This is a thought'; that's all. Thoughts come, thoughts go; emotions come, emotions go; we don't react; we just let it be, and we relax. We relax in that thought; we relax in that emotion. We just be; just rest in the present moment. We don't have to do anything about it; just be here, be present.

If we are able to do that then we will gain the confidence of being in control. At the moment we are controlled by our thoughts and emotions. Our thoughts and emotions and memories are completely overpowering us; we have no control whatsoever. That's why we suffer, why we have all the tension, the pressure, the anxiety, the problems. So we don't let that happen; we just relax and let be. And the moment we learn this, how to be, the thoughts and emotions will no longer disturb us; we will have the confidence that whatever comes up in the mind, we can let it go.

Then we will gain the confidence that we are under our own control; we are in control of the emotions and feelings, they are not in control of us. And when that happens, we are in charge! Maybe it's not so easy, but we try to go in this direction.

We're not looking for good experiences in

meditation, wonderful or strange experiences. Maybe we'll have them too; but it doesn't matter. What we are looking for is being able to relax, being able to let the thoughts and emotions come and then to let them go without their taking over.

Finding a reference point

Sometimes we'll find we can't do it; it's too difficult because we are so much habituated in that way. Our habit, our pattern, is that a thought or emotion takes us over and we just follow along humbly. So there are many different techniques and many different ways and one can do whatever works best. But one of the most important things, in the beginning, is to have a certain reference point to which we can return when we are distracted. A thought or emotion comes, and we are taken away, and we don't notice that we have been taken away, and then suddenly we realise that our mind is no longer here but is going all around the world. Then we panic and think, 'Oh, I'm distracted; I'm not meditating; this is no good – I can't relax.' Don't do that. Simply come back, and remember the object, remember the reference point.

Sometimes people take the breathing as a reference point, because this is something very natural that we do. We just remember that we are breathing. Sometimes we focus on the breathing out; sometimes on the breathing in; sometimes on the entire process of breathing out and in. We let the mind settle on the breathing, and then just relax. If the mind is somewhere else, if it's running around, then we simply remember that the mind is settled on the breathing: nothing more, nothing less. We don't struggle. We don't say, 'Oh, that was bad; I was distracted.' We don't say anything; we just relax.

Doing that repeatedly, that is meditation. Repetition is the main factor; because that's how we learn. When we learn how to drive, how do we do it? It's not difficult to know that the accelerator is to go forward and the brake is to stop and the clutch is to change the gears; but when we actually try to do it, we can't. We find ourselves doing the opposite: when you want to press the brake you push the accelerator! But we do it again and again, and again and again, and get a little bit better, and better and better. Practice. It's the practice which really makes us learn: it's the only way. Meditation is practising. First you need to learn how to do it, and then after you've learnt how to do it, you keep on doing it. There is no other way.

Taking the meditation into our daily life

The meditation period is a training session: it must be taken as a training session so that we can carry a little bit of the ease and the

releasing of tension that we learned during our meditation into our everyday life.

The more we are able to relax then the better we can feel our meditation is working; but then it's not a matter of just fifteen minutes' meditation - and finished! I think that wouldn't lead to very good results; although it might be better than not doing anything.

If we really want to carry this understanding of relaxation into our life then we have to make use of it as a way of life. We need to relax within ourselves. I don't think we need to slacken the pace of our doing things. Suppose we are very busy, with many commitments. Of course it's better not to promise too much; if we promise what we can't deliver then we're in trouble anyway; but whatever the pressures of our life, we can relax within that, we can have a little ease in our mind. Why are we trying so hard? Why are we working so hard in the first place? We are working hard in order to make ourselves happy, to make ourselves a good living. But if we work ourselves into a breakdown, then what's the use?

So trying to relax, even if we are working hard, I think is important: just letting our mind relax at the deepest level; seeing that if we are not relaxed then we can't work properly, we'll become sick or break down, and then nothing will be achieved. We need a little bit of relaxation and spaciousness in our lives; we need to bring in a little bit of this sense of being in the present moment. Most of the time it's not the work which is really giving us stress; it's the thinking about it giving us the stress. So if we can relax and be more in the present moment, then I think there will be less stress and less pressure; we can have a little bit of the taste, the lingering effect of the meditation throughout the day. And maybe we can go even further and become even better; but that is the first step.

Insight is the heart of Buddhism

The real thing is to go into the true nature of reality; that's where the insight meditation comes in. That is actually the heart of Buddhism: the insight; seeing the true nature of the mind and being able to realise it completely. It is seeing who or what we really are in a complete way.

If we can directly perceive the true, unveiled state of our mind, then that is enlightenment, that is the true freedom. Then we will cease to have any fear of anything. We don't need to feel insecure.

Insecurity and fear and all our anxieties come from the feeling that there is something to protect, something that can be damaged or lost; that there is something which is unfulfilled. But if we really know that there is nothing which is unfulfilled, and there is nothing to be secured because there is nothing to be destroyed, then we don't need to fear anything. And when you don't need to fear anything, there is no more problem. That's the transformation of our way of seeing.

The state of mind where there is fear and insecurity, where all the time we are trying to run after something or run away from something, so there is always tension and anxiety - that's called the samsaric state of mind; it's always in tension, and always unfulfilled.

The state of mind which is beyond that, where there is no more need of running, where there is the freedom which has no fear, that's called the enlightened state of mind. We call it enlightenment because it is insight: it is something that we can see, we can understand. Sometimes we call it realisation: realisation because something that we didn't realise before we realise now; it's just a matter of insight. That's why this kind of meditation is called insight meditation.

And all the many different kinds of meditation to be found in Buddhism are actually only of these two types: calm-abiding meditation and insight meditation; just these two.

Discussion

Questioner: What is the best way to deal with the strong and even painful emotions which sometimes come up during meditation?

Rinpoche: That is the meditation. Don't be afraid of facing them. Whatever comes up: anxiety, or grief or what-ever, that's where you learn how to let it be. That is where you rest, in that state of whatever is coming up; that is the main thing. The best way is not to hold on to them. It's important to understand that every emotion is a momentary thing.

Questioner: Should one encourage these emotions to come up?

Rinpoche: You don't have to encourage the emotions to come up. They come up anyway: good emotions, bad emotions; pleasant and unpleasant. Thoughts come up: all different kinds of thoughts. And when they do come up, this is the way you work. You don't say, 'Oh this shouldn't come.' It's no good doing that, because it will come up anyway. Whether you meditate or don't meditate it comes up anyway. But in meditation, because you are more rested, more comes up and you are more aware of it. The coming up is not the important thing; the important thing is learning how to let it go; that's the main exercise, that's the meditation. This is something one needs to learn. You have to just do it; keep doing it and keep trying.

But when an emotion comes up, don't think that an emotion is a lasting thing. It's not lasting; it's momentary. So you can be in that moment, there with that emotion, and just rest in the present moment. Everything that comes up is naturally momentary, coming up and coming up and coming up; so that's the first thing to realise: it's not a lasting thing. It may come up many times: the more you think about it the more it comes, and the more you follow it the more it comes. But how long it continues to come up depends on you: as long as you don't let it go, it will be there.

So when a thought or emotion comes up, whatever it is, just at that moment you relax into it, and it goes away; then another comes up, and you do the same; and another comes up, and you do the same. That's how to do the practice: with a little bit of understanding of how to do it, and then learning, and then you have to do it.

It's like learning to ride a bicycle! First you have to lose the fear of doing it; and then you have to do it. Get on, and fall down, and get some bruises; but then you'll be all right! Nobody can really tell you how to ride a bicycle, can they? People can tell you all sorts of things, but they don't really help. Somebody says, 'Why don't you just get on?' And somebody else says, 'Oh, you just hold on to the handlebars and go ahead!' And then they say, 'You have to pedal,' and, 'You have to ring the bell.' I never learned how to ride a bicycle, but I tried to learn how to ride a scooter - not very successfully! It was in Sikkim, and Sikkim is very hilly, all ups and downs; there's no flat land anywhere, not even a patch big enough to play football. So I was going this way and that on my scooter, and falling into the ditches - just when I am thinking, 'Oh no, I mustn't go into the ditch,' the scooter goes and falls precisely into the ditch! Just like our mind! But then I decided to go up to the top of the hill. I went up all right, but when I was coming down ...! The road was narrow, and there were many big army lorries; and the army drivers have come up from the plains, and they don't know how to drive in the hills - they just drive in the middle of the road. I was coming down, and an army lorry was coming up, and there were two people walking side by side... I tried sounding the horn. Nobody took any notice: a little motor scooter - nobody cares! So I tried applying the brake; but the slower you go, the more difficult it becomes to balance. And then I fell off.

And the lorry went over my scooter! That was the end of my scooter driving. But the really annoying thing was, that was the day I was planning to sell the scooter! So it's the same way; we have to learn by practice.

Questioner: What about the practice of using our own problems to develop compassion for others? If painful emotions come up in our meditation couldn't we think of others who have similar pain, and so develop our compassion?

Rinpoche: That's a good practice, but it's a different kind of meditation. When you try to rest and let your mind settle down then you don't do that practice; if you do that it will take you into more and more thoughts. But, working on a different level, it can be helpful to have a sense of perspective about our own difficulties. Usually, when we have pain, we think, 'I'm the only one suffering,' and even feel, 'I'm in a worse situation than everyone else,' and then we really suffer. But it's all very comparative, isn't it? You suffer very much because you think the worst things are coming to you, but if you see that others are actually suffering even more, then you don't feel quite so bad.

There's a story I like which illustrates this very well. There was once a man who had a big family. He and his wife had many children, and his wife's parents were living with them, and they were all in one small house. It was all very congested and he felt altogether too put upon. So the man goes to his priest and says, 'Please help me; I'm going mad! There are so many people at home and the children are running about and fighting and my wife and my in-laws are shouting and it's all too much. It's driving me crazy! What can I do?' And the priest says, 'All right. If you do exactly as I say, you can get out of it.' He says, 'Oh, I'll do anything you say - anything!' So the priest tells him: 'All right. Go and buy a chicken – a live one – and take it home.' The man goes to the market and buys a live chicken and takes it home. And of course it's even worse! He can't bear it for more than a week. He runs back to the priest and says, 'Now what can I do? It's much worse than before: the chicken is playing with the children and it's making everything dirty and it's all so much worse. What can I do?' 'Oh, don't worry,' says the priest. 'If you do exactly as I say you'll be all right. Now go and buy a goat, and take it home with you.' So he buys a goat and takes it home. And then of course it's completely chaotic, and he can't stand it for even three days before he goes back to the priest, crying, and he sobs, 'I can't bear it any longer. It's completely impossible. Whatever shall I do?' The priest tells him: 'Now you go back, and sell the goat.' So he goes back and sells the goat. And then after one week he comes to the priest and says, 'Oh, I'm so relieved. It's so peaceful now.' And the priest says, 'Now get rid of the chicken too.' So he gets rid of the chicken too (maybe makes nice chicken soup; I don't know!). Then some time later he runs into the priest in the street and says to him, 'Oh, thank you so much for your help. Now everything is quite all right!'

It can be like that, can't it? Sometimes when people say to me, 'Oh everything is so bad here; my future is so gloomy,' I suggest, 'Maybe you should go to India and have a look round.' And sometimes they go, and when they come back they say, 'Oh, it's good to be back; it's so nice here!'

So when we can think of other people who are suffering more and have even worse problems, it can help quite a lot to put our own problems into perspective. And it's also a way to develop compassion: because I don't like having problems and sufferings, therefore

I know that others who are having problems and sufferings also don't like it; and as much as I want to get out of my problems, others also want to get out of their problems too; therefore I wish that they may become free of their sufferings. This process of empathy is the main source of compassion, isn't it?

Questioner: I experience a lot of joy arising from my meditation practice, and my problem is that I'm too happy; I find this makes it difficult to get on with ordinary people in everyday life.

Rinpoche: I used to think that if something good happens to you, then you should share it with your friends and they would be very happy. But I learned from hard experience, that's not the case! If you talk about how well you're doing, it doesn't necessarily make your friends happy! So a long time ago I stopped telling my friends about the good things happening in my life; I talk instead about the problems I'm having – even if I'm not having many problems. Now I seem to get on better with my friends! They understand it as, 'He has problems too, just like me.'

I think that if you want to get along with people it's important to be able to see things from their point of view and put yourself in their shoes, so you can understand them; and the more you understand people and how they are feeling, the more you know how to be with them - and sometimes, I think, it's all right to pretend a little if necessary.

Questioner: Is it helpful to identify and note the emotions coming up in meditation, for example, 'This is anger; this is attachment etc'?

Rinpoche: That's maybe another technique. If you are just trying to do this calming down meditation it's better not to make labels too much. If you make labels it can lead to too much thinking. First you say, 'I'm feeling this'; then comes 'this is good' or 'this is bad'; then 'I don't like it' or 'I like it'; and then the next thing is 'this should not be' or 'this should be'; and then you can get more and more into that kind of stream of thought and lose the meditation. So I think it's better not to do that; perhaps be a little bit aware of what's going on, but don't put too much emphasis on that. The more quickly you can let it be, the better.

Questioner: When I first began meditating some time ago I used to get very positive experiences, but after a while they stopped happening and now I haven't had any good experiences for a long time. Does this mean progress has stopped?

Rinpoche: I think that is very normal. When you start to practice, many experiences may come. Then at a certain stage you no longer have them, and then at another stage it even becomes difficult to meditate, and you seem to make progress very slowly. I think that's true of almost anything you learn, isn't it? Even learning a language: for the first few months you will see yourself progressing very quickly. Yesterday you didn't even know how to say hello and today you learn how to say not only 'Hello' but also 'Thank you very much'! And next day you learn 'How are you?'! But after some time you don't seem to be learning much, and you can't see any progress. It's always like that: when you start there's a steep rate of progress, but then of course it levels off; it's not always a steady upward trend.

From the traditional point of view it is said that one's progress in meditation falls into five stages. The first stage of progress is like a waterfall: the water in the waterfall is rushing down with full force; so it's as though your thoughts and emotions are becoming very forceful like rushing water, and it's almost as if you cannot meditate any more. That is regarded as the first proper stage; a sign that you are progressing in meditation. In other words: if you feel you can't meditate at all, then you are going to be a great meditator!

Meditation experiences sometimes come early, sometimes later, but they come and go. Usually these kinds of fleeting experiences, which are called nyam (nyams) in Tibetan, are not regarded as very important from the point of view of real meditators. Good experiences in meditation are not the main thing to look forward to. If you have a good experience, you'll want to have it again, and the moment you want it and try to have it again, you can't get it; you have this good experience because you have completely relaxed, and when you try to have it, you can't! The more you want it, the less likely you are to get it – and then you get frustrated! So all the meditation masters emphasise that you shouldn't take this kind of experience too seriously. It's a nice experience but it comes and goes, and we shouldn't have too much attachment to it. It's the same with bad experiences: the masters tell us that a bad experience and a good experience are exactly the same. Bad experience, good experience; no good experience, no bad experience; all are the same. It's all just experience.

The real meditation is to be able to learn that whatever experience arises, it doesn't matter; it's just an experience, and you can relax in that. If it's a good experience, you learn to relax in that; if it's a bad experience, you learn to relax in that; if it's neither a good nor a bad experience, you learn to relax in that.

If you learn how to do that in all these three different cases then you have learned how to meditate.

Thank you all very much.

All my babbling,
In the name of Dharma
Has been set down faithfully
By my dear students of pure vision.

I pray that at least a fraction of the wisdom
Of those enlightened teachers
Who tirelessly trained me
Shines through this mass of incoherence.

May the sincere efforts of all those
Who have worked tirelessly
Result in spreading the true meaning of Dharma
To all who are inspired to know.

May this help dispel the darkness of ignorance
In the minds of all living beings
And lead them to complete realisation
Free from all fear.

Ringu Tulku

Acknowledgements

We would like to thank the students of Chime Rinpoche at Marpa House who hosted the talk and posed the questions in this book.

We also wish to thank the original team that produced the first edition of this book: Jean Beverton, for design and layout; Robin Bath, for his drawings; Norma Levine, for her advice on editing; Alison de Ledesma, for distribution; and Cait Collins, for transcribing and editing this book.

For this second edition we would like to thank: Paul O'Connor, for this new layout and design; Dr Dirk de Klerk, for the cover photo; Dr Conrad Harvey & Rebecca O'Connor, for the new Lazy Lama logo illustration; and Annie Dibble, for proof reading.

About the Author

Ringu Tulku Rinpoche is a Tibetan Buddhist Master of the Kagyu Order. He was trained in all schools of Tibetan Buddhism under many great masters including HH the 16th Gyalwang Karmapa and HH Dilgo Khyentse Rinpoche. He took his formal education at Namgyal Institute of Tibetology, Sikkim and Sampurnananda Sanskrit University, Varanasi, India. He served as Tibetan Textbook Writer and Professor of Tibetan Studies in Sikkim for 25 years.

Since 1990, he has been travelling and teaching Buddhism and meditation in Europe, America, Canada, Australia and Asia. He participates in various interfaith and 'Science and Buddhism' dialogues and is the author of several books on Buddhist topics. These include Path to Buddhahood, Daring Steps, The Ri-me Philosophy of Jamgon Kongtrul the

Great, Confusion Arises as Wisdom, the Lazy Lama series and the Heart Wisdom series, as well as several children's books, available in Tibetan and European languages.

He founded the organisations:
Bodhicharya - see www.bodhicharya.org
and Rigul Trust - see www.rigultrust.org

Other books by Bodhicharya Publications

The Lazy Lama Series:

No. 1 - Buddhist Meditation

No. 2 - The Four Noble Truths

No. 3 - Refuge: Finding a Purpose and a Path

No. 4 - Bodhichitta: Awakening Compassion and Wisdom

No. 5 - Living without Fear and Anger

Heart Wisdom Series:

The Ngöndro: *Foundation Practices of Mahamudra*

From Milk to Yoghurt: *A Recipe for Living and Dying*

Like Dreams and Clouds: *Emptiness and Interdependence; Mahamudra and Dzogchen*

Dealing with Emotions: *Scattering the Clouds*

Journey from Head to Heart: *Along a Buddhist Path*

See: www.bodhicharya.org/publications

Rigul TrusT

Patron: Ringu Tulku Rinpoche

Rigul Trust is a UK charity whose objectives are the relief of poverty and financial hardship, the advancement of education, the advancement of religion, the relief of sickness, the preservation of good health.

Our main project is helping with health and education in Rigul, Tibet, the homeland of Ringu Tulku Rinpoche where his monastery is. We currently fund Dr Chuga, the nurse, the doctor's assistant, the running costs of the health clinic, the teachers, the cooks and the children's education plus two, free, hot meals a day at school.

We also help raise funds for disasters like earthquakes, floods, and help with schools in India and other health and welfare projects. All administration costs are met privately by volunteers.

100% OF ALL DONATIONS GOES TO FUND HEALTH, EDUCATION AND POVERTY RELIEF PROJECTS

Rigul Trust

13 St. Francis Avenue, Southampton, SO18 5QL U.K.

info@rigultrust.org

UK Charity Registration No: 1124076

TO FIND OUT MORE, OR MAKE A DONATION, PLEASE VISIT:

www.rigultrust.org

For an up to date list of books by Ringu Tulku,
please see the Books section at

www.bodhicharya.org

*All proceeds received by Bodhicharya Publications
from the sale of this book go direct to humanitarian
and educational projects because the work involved in
producing this book has been given free of charge.*